the illustrated

*B*OOK *of* WISDOM

Peace &
Serenity

SILVERLEAF
PRESS

Peace of mind is attained

NOT BY IGNORING PROBLEMS,

but by

SOLVING THEM.

RAYMOND HULL

I F I HAVE BEEN OF SERVICE,
if I have glimpsed more of the
nature and essence of ultimate
good, if I am inspired to reach
wider horizons of thought and
action, if I am at peace with
myself, it has been
a successful day.

Alex Noble

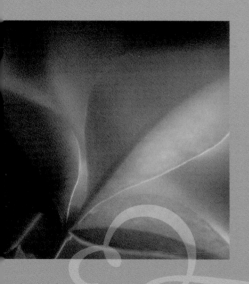

Serenity is the last lesson of culture, the fruitage of the soul. It is precious as wisdom, more to be desired than gold.

JAMES ALLEN

PEACE IN

OURSELVES

Ultimately, we have just one moral duty:
to reclaim large areas of peace in ourselves,
more and more peace, and to reflect it
toward others. And the more peace there
is in us, the more peace there will also be
in our troubled world.

Etty Hillesum

*Peace is not something
you wish for; it's something
you make, something you
do, something you are,
something you give away.*

ROBERT FULGHUM

SOMETHING
YOU GIVE AWAY

Silence fertilizes the deep place

where personality grows.

A life with a peaceful center

can weather all storms.

Norman Vincent Peale

A peaceful center

POWER FOR GOOD

The more tranquil
a man becomes,
the greater is his success,
his influence,
his power for good.

James Allen

What I dream of is an art of balance, of purity and serenity devoid of troubling or depressing subject matter—a soothing, calming influence on the mind, rather like a good armchair which provides relaxation from physical fatigue.

Henri Matisse

INNER PEACE

*N*ever be in a hurry;
do everything quietly and in a
calm spirit. Do not lose your
inner peace for anything
whatsoever, even if your
whole world seems upset.

ST. FRANCIS DE SALES

*Always direct
your thoughts to those
truths that will give you
confidence, hope, joy,
love, thanksgiving, and
turn away your mind
from those that inspire
you with fear, sadness,
depression.*

BERTRAND WILBERTFORCE

CHANGE YOURSELF

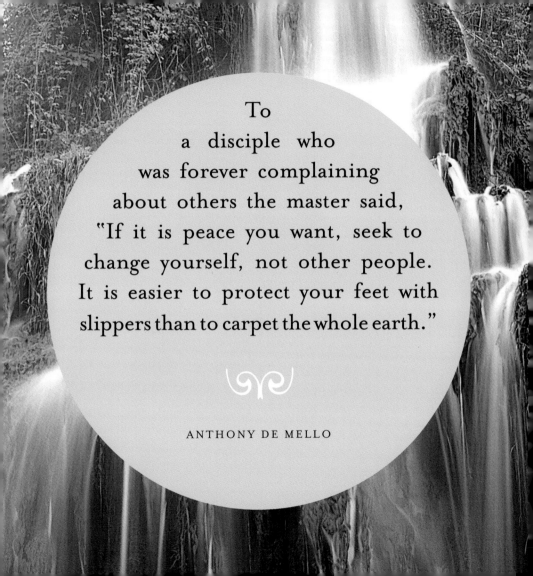

To
a disciple who
was forever complaining
about others the master said,
"If it is peace you want, seek to
change yourself, not other people.
It is easier to protect your feet with
slippers than to carpet the whole earth."

ANTHONY DE MELLO

THE GREATEST REVOLUTION

*T*he greatest
revolution in our generation
is the discovery that human
beings, by changing the inner
attitudes of their minds, can
change the outer aspects
of their lives.

William James

To live continually in thoughts

of ill-will, cynicism, suspicion, and envy, is to be confined

in a self-made prison hole. But to think well of all, to be

cheerful with all, to patiently learn to find the good in all—

such unselfish thoughts are the very portals of heaven;

and to dwell day by day in thoughts of peace toward every

creature will bring abounding peace to their possessor.

James Allen

The LAW of NATURE

THERE IS A WONDERFUL mythical law of

nature that the three things we crave most in

life—happiness, freedom, and peace of

mind—are always attained by giving

them to someone else.

PEYTON CONWAY MARCH

Great tranquility of heart is his

who cares for neither

praise nor blame.

Thomas à Kempis

WORRY DOES NOT
EMPTY TOMORROW OF ITS SORROWS, IT EMPTIES
TODAY OF ITS STRENGTH.

Corrie Ten Boom

Triumph of

Principles

A political victory, a rise in rents, the recovery of your sick, or return of your absent friend, or some other quite external event, raises your spirits, and you think good days are preparing for you. Do not believe it. Nothing can bring you peace but yourself. Nothing can bring you peace but the triumph of principles.

❖❖❖❖❖❖❖❖

Ralph Waldo Emerson

FILL YOUR MIND *with the meaningless stimuli of a world preoccupied with meaningless things, and it will not be easy to feel peace in your heart.*

MARIANNE WILLIAMSON

*W*e can easily manage if we will only take, each day, the burden appointed to it. But the load will be too heavy for us if we carry yesterday's burden over again today, and then add the burden of the morrow before we are required to bear it.

John Newton

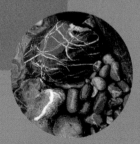

* * * * * * A man becomes calm in the measure that he understands himself as a thought-evolved being. For such knowledge necessitates the understanding of others as the result of thought, and as he develops a right understanding, and sees ever more clearly the internal relations of things by the action of cause and effect, he ceases to fuss, fume, worry, and grieve. He remains poised, steadfast, serene.

James Allen

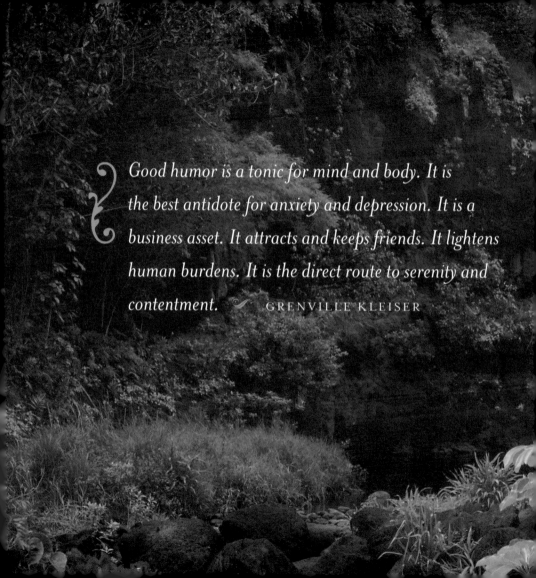

Good humor is a tonic for mind and body. It is the best antidote for anxiety and depression. It is a business asset. It attracts and keeps friends. It lightens human burdens. It is the direct route to serenity and contentment. GRENVILLE KLEISER

INTEGRITY

OF MIND

Nothing is at last sacred but the integrity of your own mind. Absolve you to yourself, and you shall have the suffrage of the world.... No law can be sacred to me but that of my nature. Good and bad are but names very readily transferable to that or this; the only right is what is after my constitution, the only wrong what is against it. A man is to carry himself in the presence of all opposition, as if every thing were titular and ephemeral but he.

Ralph Waldo Emerson

The strong, calm man is always loved and revered. He is like a shade-giving tree in a thirsty land, or a sheltering rock in a storm. Who does not love a tranquil heart, a sweet-tempered, balanced life? It does not matter whether it rains or shines, or what changes come to those possessing these blessings, for they are always sweet, serene, and calm.

James Allen

SEARCH WITHIN

People spend a lifetime searching for happiness; looking for peace. They chase idle dreams, addictions, religions, even other people, hoping to fill the emptiness that plagues them. The irony is the only place they ever needed to search was within.

Ramona L. Anderson

There are hundreds of
tasks we feel we must
accomplish in the day,
but if we do not take them
one at a time and let them
pass through the day
slowly and evenly, as do
the grains of sand passing
through the narrow neck
of the hourglass, then we
are bound to break our
own physical and mental
structure.

Ted Bergernine

ONE AT A TIME

When one has found peace within himself, its radiance will pervade his home, his neighborhood, and, in an ever-widening circle, flavor and color every life he touches.

HUGH B. BROWN

right in the moment

EVERY DAY WE DO THINGS, WE ARE THINGS THAT HAVE TO DO WITH PEACE. IF WE ARE AWARE OF OUR LIFE...OUR WAY OF LOOKING AT THINGS, WE WILL KNOW HOW TO MAKE PEACE RIGHT IN THE MOMENT, WE ARE ALIVE.

Thich Nhat Hanh

I KEEP THE TELEPHONE
of my mind open to peace, harmony,
health, love and abundance. Then
whenever doubt, anxiety, or fear try to call
me, they keep getting a busy signal and
soon they'll forget my number.

❦ *Edith Armstrong* ❦

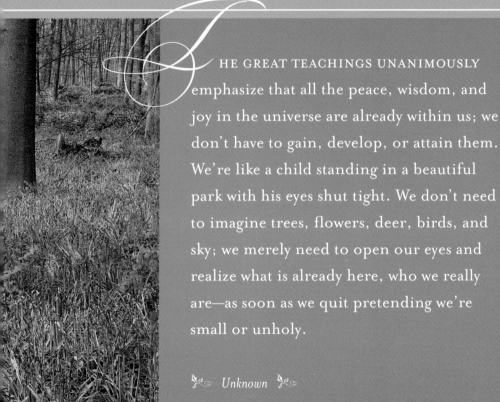

THE GREAT TEACHINGS UNANIMOUSLY emphasize that all the peace, wisdom, and joy in the universe are already within us; we don't have to gain, develop, or attain them. We're like a child standing in a beautiful park with his eyes shut tight. We don't need to imagine trees, flowers, deer, birds, and sky; we merely need to open our eyes and realize what is already here, who we really are—as soon as we quit pretending we're small or unholy.

Unknown

TRANQUILITY

The poor long for riches, the rich long for heaven, but the wise long for a state of tranquility.

Swami Rama

INNER PEACE

*R*esponsibility does not only lie with the leaders of our countries or with those who have been appointed or elected to do a particular job. It lies with each of us individually. Peace, for example, starts within each one of us. When we have inner peace, we can be at peace with those around us.

DALAI LAMA

Five enemies of
peace inhabit with us—avarice, ambition, envy, anger, and pride; if these were to be banished, we should infallibly enjoy perpetual peace.

 Petrarch

If pain for peace prepares,
Lo the "Augustan" years
    Our feet await!

If Springs from Winter rise,
Can the Anemone's
    Be reckoned up?

If night stands first, then noon,
To gird us for the sun,
    What gaze—

When, from a thousand skies,
On our developed eyes
    Noons blaze!

Emily Dickinson

NOONS BLAZE

ONE HABIT THAT PREVENTS INNER PEACE
IS PROCRASTINATION. IT CLUTTERS OUR
MINDS WITH UNFINISHED BUSINESS
AND MAKES US UNEASY UNTIL WE FINISH
A TASK AND GET IT OUT OF THE WAY.

Joseph B. Wirthlin

You cannot perceive
beauty but with a
serene mind.

Henry David Thoreau

in quiet waters

ONLY

*in quiet
waters do
things mirror
themselves
undistorted.
Only in a
quiet mind
is adequate
perception of
the world.*

HANS MARGOLIUS

Calmness of mind

is one of the beautiful

jewels of wisdom.

It is the result of long and

patient effort in self-control.

JAMES ALLEN

CLIMB THE
mountains and get their
good tidings. Nature's peace will
flow into you as sunshine
flows into trees.
The winds will blow their own
freshness into you,
and the storms their energy,
while cares will drop off
like autumn leaves.

❖ ❖ ❖

John Muir

like autumn leaves

$\mathcal{T}$o attain inner peace you must actually give your life, not just your possessions. When you at last give your life—bringing into alignment your beliefs and the way you live then, and only then, can you begin to find inner peace.

Peace Pilgrim

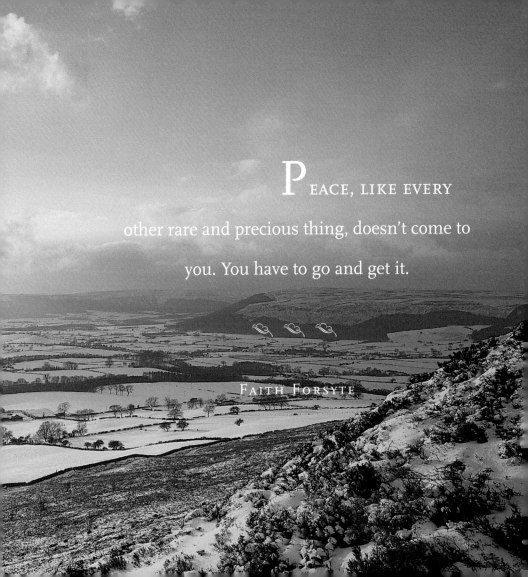

PEACE, LIKE EVERY

other rare and precious thing, doesn't come to

you. You have to go and get it.

FAITH FORSYTE

While conscience is our friend, all is at peace; however once it is offended, farewell to a tranquil mind.

Lady Mary Wortley Montagu

HOLY HEARTS

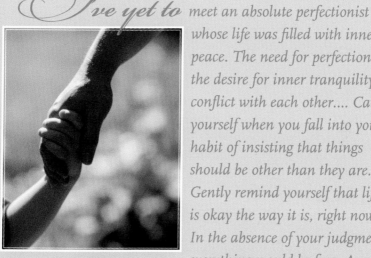

I've yet to meet an absolute perfectionist
whose life was filled with inner
peace. The need for perfection and
the desire for inner tranquility
conflict with each other.... Catch
yourself when you fall into your
habit of insisting that things
should be other than they are.
Gently remind yourself that life
is okay the way it is, right now.
In the absence of your judgment,
everything would be fine. As you
begin to eliminate your need for
perfection in all areas of your
life, you'll begin to discover the
perfection in life itself.

Richard Carlson

SUPREMACY OVER FEAR

$\mathcal{P}$eace is when you can turn a corner without apprehension and look in the eye those you meet; it is the supremacy over fear, not fearlessness, but the courage to go forward in spite of fear; it is the hearing of the telephone bell without a start; the opening of your door to the police without a quiver; the receiving of a telegram without a tremble.

Spencer W. Kimball

*T*he glory of a good man is the testimony of a good conscience. Therefore, keep your conscience good and you will always enjoy happiness, for a good conscience can bear a great deal and can bring joy even in the midst of adversity. But an evil conscience is ever restive and fearful. Sweet shall be your rest if your heart does not reproach you.

THOMAS À KEMPIS

Whenever conscience speaks with a divided, uncertain, and disputed voice, it is not the voice of God. Descend still deeper into yourself, until you hear nothing but a clear, undivided voice, a voice which does away with doubt and brings with it persuasion, light, and serenity.

 HENRI F. AMIEL

Everybody today seems to be in such a terrible rush;

anxious for greater developments and greater wishes and so on;

so that children have very little time for their parents;

parents have very little time for each other;

and in the home begins the disruption of the peace of the world.

 Mother Teresa

{ constant serenity }

A GOOD CONSCIENCE IS TO THE
SOUL WHAT HEALTH IS TO THE BODY;
IT PRESERVES CONSTANT EASE AND
SERENITY WITHIN US; AND MORE
THAN COUNTERVAILS ALL THE
CALAMITIES AND AFFLICTIONS WHICH
CAN BEFALL US FROM WITHOUT.

Joseph Addison

W HATEVER YOU DO,
you need courage. Whatever
course you decide upon, there
is always someone to tell you
that you are wrong. There are
always difficulties arising that
tempt you to believe your critics
are right. To map out a course
of action and follow it to an
end requires some of the same
courage that a soldier needs.
Peace has its victories, but it
takes brave men and women
to win them.

RALPH WALDO EMERSON

Symptoms of Inner Peace

- *A tendency to think and act spontaneously rather than on fears based on past experience*
- *An unmistakable ability to enjoy the moment*
- *A loss of interest in judging other people*
- *A loss of interest in judging self*
- *A loss of interest in interpreting the actions of others*
- *A loss of interest in conflict*
- *An inability to worry (this is a very serious symptom!)*
- *Frequent overwhelming episodes of appreciation*
- *Contented feelings of connectedness with others and nature*
- *Frequent acts of smiling*
- *An increasing tendency to let things happen rather than to make them happen*
- *An increased susceptibility to the love extended by others as well as the uncontrollable urge to extend it*

☼ Anonymous

Silverleaf Press books are available exclusively
through Independent Publishers Group.

For details write or telephone
Independent Publishers Group,
814 North Franklin St.
Chicago, IL 60610, (312) 337-0747.

Silverleaf Press
8160 South Highland Drive
Sandy, Utah 84093

Book design by Andy Goddard

ISBN 1-933317-12-4

Printed in Malaysia
1 2 3 4 5 6 7 8 9 10